BALD EAGLES

BALD EAGLES

SANDRA LEE

T H E   C H I L D ' S   W O R L D

DESIGN
Bill Foster of Albarella & Associates, Inc.

PHOTO CREDITS
Tom and Pat Leeson: front cover, back cover, 2, 6,
8, 12, 15, 16, 19, 25, 29, 31
Lon E. Lauber/Aleutian Photographic: 10, 21, 23
W. Perry Conway: 26

Distributed to schools and libraries
in the United States by
ENCYCLOPAEDIA BRITANNICA EDUCATIONAL CORP
310 South Michigan Ave.
Chicago, Illinois 60604

Library of Congress Cataloging-in-Publication Data
Lee, Sandra.
Bald Eagles/Sandra Lee.
p. cm. — (Child's World Wildlife Library)
Summary: Describes the characteristics and habits of the bird
chosen as the national emblem of the United States.
ISBN 0-89565-706-6
1. Bald eagle — Juvenile literature.
[1. Bald eagle.   2. Eagles.]   I. Title.
II. Series.   91-12519
QL696.F32L43 1991   CIP
598.9'16—dc20   AC

Dedicated to those who helped save the bald eagle from extinction

The bald eagle is one of the most familiar of all birds. Its flight is majestic, especially as the eagle swoops or soars. At close range it looks fierce and proud. Throughout history it has been used as a symbol of power and freedom.

The bald eagle is actually not bald, as its name suggests. It only looks bald because of the snow-white feathers on its head and neck. The rest of its body is either black or dark brown.

Bald eagles are not as big as many people imagine. Adult eagles grow to about three feet long, which includes their long tail feathers. They weigh only 8 to 13 pounds — about the same as an average house cat.

Although their bodies are not very large, eagles do have strong, broad wings. Their spread wings measure from six to eight feet. That's nearly twice as long as your outstretched arms. The large wings easily support the eagle's body when it flies. By holding the wings out stiffly, the bird can glide for hours. Its feathers spread out like fingers as it soars.

Bald eagles live near rivers, lakes, and seacoasts. They spend much of their time roosting in tall trees. They sit perfectly quiet, appearing asleep. In fact, they are watching everything around them. An eagle's vision is about eight times sharper than a person's. An eagle can see a mouse from nearly a mile away.

Despite their reputation, bald eagles are not very good hunters. They feed mainly on fish and dead animals. Eagles have strong feet, armed with long, curved claws called *talons*. They often use their sharp talons to steal fish from other birds. Eagles also use their talons to catch their own fish.

When fishing, an eagle dips its talons into the water and snags a fish that is swimming close to the surface. The eagle tries not to get its feathers wet. If its feathers get too wet the eagle cannot take off from the water and may drown.

After catching a fish, the eagle carries its meal to a treetop, where it can eat without being bothered. After a large meal, an eagle may not eat again for a day or two.

Eagles choose one mate for life. The eagle pair builds a nest in the top of a tree or a cliff near water. The nest, called an *eyrie*, is built with sticks and lined with moss, grass, and leaves. The eagles return to the same nest every spring and add new materials. Each year the eyrie becomes bigger and bigger. An old eyrie may be 10, 12, or even 20 feet across!

In May or June, the female eagle lays her eggs.

Usually, she lays two eggs at a time. Both parents

take turns sitting on the eggs to keep them warm.

About a month after the eggs are laid, the chicks

inside break out of their shells. The chicks, called

eaglets, are covered with white, fluffy down.

The eaglets grow fast. The parents have to work hard to satisfy their big appetites. After about two months, the eaglet's white down is replaced by dark brown feathers. The white head feathers do not come until much later.

The eaglets learn to fly when they are about three months old. At first, the young birds exercise their wing muscles by jumping and flapping their wings. Then they finally make the leap from their treetop perch. The eaglets cannot fly very well at first. They stay near the eyrie for several weeks and continue to sleep there. The parents continue to feed their young for several months.

Eagles develop their adult feathers when they are about four to five years old. By that time, they are ready to choose a mate and build their own nests. Eagles often build their eyries within 100 miles of where they were raised. In the wild, bald eagles may live for 20 to 30 years. They can live for 50 years or longer if they are kept in a zoo or some other protected area.

Not too long ago, eagles were becoming very scarce. They were dying because of a chemical called DDT. Farmers and other people used DDT to kill bugs. The DDT washed into rivers and lakes, where fish were poisoned by it. Since eagles eat a lot of fish, the poison collected in their bodies, too. It made the eagles' eggshells very thin. When the adult eagles sat on the eggs to keep them warm, the shells would crack and the chicks growing inside would die.

After scientists discovered the harmful effects of DDT, laws were passed to stop its use. Laws also protect eagles from hunters in all states. Thanks to these efforts, the eagle population is gradually increasing. Today, there are more eagles than there have been for many years.

The eagle is familiar to Americans because we see it so often: on quarters, dollar bills, and stamps. However, not everyone is lucky enough to see a bald eagle in the wild. When one does, it is a sight to remember. Because of the efforts of so many concerned people, we are now more likely to see eagles in their natural surroundings.